The Sampling Distri
Central Limit Theor
"In Plain English"

By Douglas Brooks, PhD

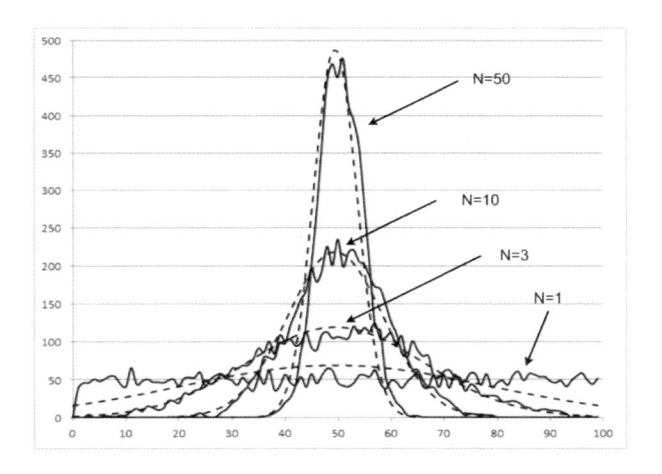

Copyrights and Trademarks 2012 by Douglas Brooks, Kirkland, WA,
And UltraCAD Design, Inc. Bellevue, WA.

Copyright 2012 by:
Douglas G. Brooks, PhD
Kirkland, WA 98033

TABLE OF CONTENTS

1.0 Introduction:
2.0 Distributions
    2.1 Population Distribution:
    2.2 Sample Distribution
    2.3 Sampling Distribution
3.0 Central Limit Theorem:
    3.1 An Example:
        3.1.1 With replacement:
        3.1.2 Without replacement:
    3.2 Back to the Example.
    3.3 The Normal Curve:
4. Sample Size:
    4.1 For Normal Approximation:
    4.2 For Sufficient Precision:
5. Another Example:
6. Extension to Proportions:
    6.1 Margin of Error:

Appendix 1
About the Author

The Sampling Distribution and Central Limit Theorem
"In Plain English"

Introduction:

Ahhh... the power of statistics! Suppose I want to know the average weight of the shipping containers that pass through a shipping terminal. I don't have any idea what that average weight is. I don't even have any idea how many shipping containers there are in the population I am thinking about (all the shipping containers that pass through the terminal.) In statistical terms, I don't know the size of the population, the mean of the population, or anything about the distribution of the weights within the population (this last variable relates to "variance" and "standard deviation.")

So I take a sample. And from it I determine the mean weight of the sample (call it x-bar for now) and the variance of the sample. OK. So what? What does the sample *really* tell me about the population? Well, if I have done things correctly (i.e. if my sample is a truly random one), then I can make the following statement:

I know with a 95% probability that the mean weight of the population is within +/- y pounds of x-bar.

Read that again! What it says is that I know (with 95% confidence) how close my sample mean is to the true mean, even though I have no idea what the true mean is. Or even what the population looks like! I know how close I am to the truth without knowing what the truth is! And if that's not close enough, I know what to do to get a closer estimate. Now that's pretty powerful!

The reason I can make a statement like that is because of the Central Limit Theorem. And the Central Limit Theorem applies to the Sampling Distribution. And that's what this booklet is all about.

Before we go any further, I'd like to make three general comments about writing this booklet:

1. The first relates to the Central Limit Theorem itself. I remember when I started taking Statistics, and later when I started teaching it to college students. Approximately the first half of the first course in Statistics is spent talking about basic measures related to Statistics (mean, variance, standard deviation, etc.) and about probabilities and their distributions. Then we talk about the sampling distribution and the Central Limit Theorem. Then we start looking at several different applications of Statistics (estimation, hypothesis testing, t-tests, ANOVA, regression, etc.)

The Central Limit Theorem is sort of a peak. All that first stuff builds up to the peak. Students who get over the peak --- those who really understand the sampling distribution and the Central Limit Theorem --- have very little trouble with anything that follows in Statistics (even over several follow-on courses.) But students who can't get over the peak --- those who never quite get the Central Limit Theorem and all it represents --- have trouble with *everything* that follows! The Central Limit Theorem is that fundamental to Statistics. If you get it, the field is easy. If you don't, well very little of it makes any real sense.

That is why I wrote this. The first version of this booklet was written for my students back in 1973. I am resurrecting it now in ebook and printed form in hopes that you will find it helpful.

2. Most of my students in Basic Statistics were there because they had to be there! It was a required course. And most of them had heard, and believed, it was going to be a very difficult course in mathematics. And that was a terrible misconception. From a mathematics standpoint, statistics is easy. It involves addition, subtraction, multiplication, division, and the occasional square root. All this can be done on today's spreadsheets, pocket calculators, and even most cell phones! It is not the math that is difficult.

What is difficult is that it is like (a) a course in a foreign language and (b) a course in logic. There are a large number of new definitions and symbols the student gets exposed to, especially in the first part of the first course. And most of these symbols are (literally) Greek! There are things like mu, rho, sigma (both capital sigma and lower case sigma), and sigma-x and sigma-x-bar, and sometimes the differences between them are subtle. And then there is a whole lot if "if this, then that" and "if not this then not that." It really can be confusing. Not difficult, but confusing.

3. This booklet is intended as a supplement to a basic course in Statistics. It is not intended to be a complete reference work. Therefore, it is assumed that the reader has at least been exposed, at some point, to the concepts of mean, variance, standard deviation, basic sampling procedures, and various probability distributions, especially the Normal distribution.

So here we go........

2.0 Distributions

There are three basic distributions that are of particular interest in Statistics (not discounting the importance of various probability distributions, such as the Normal curve.) They are the Population Distribution, the Sample Distribution, and the Sampl*ing* Distribution. A description of each follows:

2.1 Population Distribution:

The population distribution is the main population we are interested in. We might know something about it, but it is not necessary that we know very much. There are two types of populations we will mention in this booklet, those relating to a measure of some kind of quantity (size, weight, income, wealth, SAT score, IQ, performance measure, etc.) and those relating to a proportion (pass/fail, approve/disapprove of Congress, approve candidate A or B, etc.) A population has a size, N, which we may or may not know.

In the first type of population, we commonly use the variable X to represent each individual element we are interested in. So we can (at least conceptually) identify each element as X_1, X_2, X_3....X_N. The average (really *mean*) of the measure is given by the sum of the elements divided by the size of the population:

[Eq. 1]
$$\mu = \sum_{i=1}^{N} X_i / N$$

We probably don't know the mean. If we did, we wouldn't be talking about sampling!

The values of X spread out over a range. And the distribution is the relative frequency distribution of each X in the range. In statistical terms we use variance and standard deviation as measures of that range. The formulas look intimidating, but they are pretty straightforward. To find the variance (sigma-squared), (a) take each individual element, X, (b) subtract the mean, (c) square the result, (d) add up all these squared values, (e) then divide by the number of values (N). To find the standard deviation (sigma), take the square root of the variance. So the standard deviation is given by this formula:

$$\sigma = \sqrt{\sum_{i=1}^{N}\left((X_i - \mu)^2 / N\right)}$$

[Eq. 2]

This type of population is characterized by 4 parameters, its size (N), its mean µ, its variance σ^2, and its standard deviation σ.

The second type of population also has a size we'll call N. But instead of a mean it has a proportion we'll call p. Typically, we are interested in one proportion at a time, so there are elements of the population that are part of p, and elements that are not. The proportion of those that are not are represented by the letter q, where q=1-p. The variance of this kind of population is given by

$$\sigma^2 = pq$$

[Eq. 3]

And the standard deviation is simply the square root of the variance.

[Eq. 4] $$\sigma = \sqrt{pq}$$

Note that every population is characterized by at least four attributes, size, mean (or proportion), variance, and standard deviation. For sampling purposes it is not necessary for us to know any of these attributes.

2.2 Sample Distribution

When we draw a sample from the population, we are drawing elements from the population, the X_i's. The sample has a size, n. We refer to the elements we have drawn from the population as sample elements, and distinguish them by using lower case x_i's. The sample distribution is the relative frequency distribution of the x_i's. The sample has a mean which is calculated just like the population mean would be:

[Eq. 5] $$\overline{x} = \sum_{i=1}^{n} x_i / n$$

And it has a sample variance and standard deviation. The sample standard deviation is given by the formula:

[Eq. 6]
$$S_x = \sqrt{\sum_{i=1}^{n}(x_i - \overline{x})^2 / (n-1)}$$

Technical note: Some writers and professors will add a "finite population correction factor" to Equation 6 if we are sampling "without replacement". That factor is $\sqrt{\left(\frac{N-n}{N-1}\right)}$. Doing so is strictly correct. Other writers note that if n is sufficiently large, and if N is much larger than n (which is true in a great many practical cases), then n-1 reduces to n, and (N-n)/(N-1) reduces to one, making all the corrections trivial.

The sample is therefore characterized by four parameters, size n, mean x-bar, a variance and a standard deviation, just like the population is. And if the sample is "reasonable" size (we'll talk about this later), then the sample parameters are estimates of the population parameters. Indeed, if we have drawn the sample using good statistical procedures (i.e. we have been careful to get a *random* sample), then the sample should look a lot like the population.

Now it might not look like the population. We might, for example, been unlucky enough to draw the n lowest value elements from the population. Or perhaps the n highest value elements. But we'd have to be awfully unlucky to do that. With any luck at all, and for a reasonable sample size, our sample should resemble the population pretty closely.

2.3 Sampling Distribution

Now before we even start this discussion, it should be intuitive that the sampling distribution will be made up of elements, it will have a size, it will have a variance, and it will have a standard deviation. And it will have a shape. Let's start with the elements.

When we took a sample of size n from the population of N, and calculated a sample mean, x-bar, that was one sample we could have taken. We could have taken other samples. For example, we could have taken the n smallest members of the population. We could have taken the n largest members of the population. We could have taken the n elements closest to the population mean. Or we could have taken any other combination of elements. How many combinations are possible? In any normal practical situation the answer is a kazillion (that's a technical term that means a lot!) If we are taking a truly random sample, any one of these kazillion possible samples has an equal probability of being selected. In fact, the sample with the n smallest elements has the same probability of being selected as any other combination, 1/kazillion.

Every one of these samples has a sample mean, x-bar. Let's play a mind game and think about taking every one of the kazil-

13

lion samples and calculating the sample mean (the x-bar) of each one. That would be a kazillion x-bars. Those kazillion x-bars would have a range of values and there would be a mean of the x-bars we could calculate:

$$\text{\textit{mean} of the x-bars} = \sum_{i=1}^{kazillion} \overline{x}_i \ / \ kazillion$$

[Eq. 7]

Now here is another leap. Stop thinking about samples and their x-bars. Just think about all those x-bars. There are a kazillion of them. When we want to take a sample from the population to try to determine the mean weight of the containers in the transportation yard, what we are doing is randomly selecting one of those x-bars from the kazillion of them that are available to us. If we were really unlucky, the x-bar we select could be calculated from the smallest elements of the population. Or, it might be calculated from the largest elements of the population. But we would have to be really unlucky to select either of these. After all, there are a kazillion x-bars to select from, and each one has only one chance in a kazillion of being selected. So selecting the worst one would be really unlucky!

It is this distribution of x-bars that we call the sampling distribution. The x-bars are the elements making up this distribution. This distribution has a size (a kazillion), it has a mean (Equation 7), and it has a standard deviation. And it is the Central Limit Theorem that tells us what this distribution looks like

--- what its shape is, where it is located (i.e. what its mean is), and what its standard deviation is.

THIS IS THE PEAK I REFERENCED IN THE INTRODUCTION. If you can really grasp what the sampling distribution is --- the distribution of all the possible means, each one of which is calculated from one of all the possible samples of size n that can be taken from the population of size N --- then the rest is easy.

What does this distribution look like, where is it located, and what is its standard deviation? It is the Central Limit Theorem that answers these questions.

3.0 Central Limit Theorem:

The Central Limit Theorem tells us that, for a reasonable size n, the sampling distribution (the distribution of all the means of all the possible samples of size n) is approximated by a Normal curve whose mean is mu, the mean of the population, and whose standard deviation is the standard deviation of the population divided by the square root of the sample size, n. That is, it is a normal curve whose

[Eq. 8] $\quad$ mean of the $\bar{x}$'s $= \mu$, the mean of the population and

[Eq. 9] $$\text{standard deviation of the } \bar{x}\text{'s} = \sigma_{\bar{x}} = \sigma/\sqrt{n}$$

This means we know that the sample mean we draw from the population comes from a Normal distribution whose mean is the mean of the population (even though we don't know what that is) and whose standard deviation is the standard deviation of the population divided by the square root of the sample size. (And if you are wondering where we get the standard deviation of the population, we can possibly get that from prior studies, or we can estimate it from the standard deviation of the sample, which itself, is an estimate of the population standard deviation.)

Note that we know the shape of the sampling distribution (the distribution of the means of all the possible samples of size n) is a Normal curve, even though we have no idea what the shape of the population distribution is. And the shape of the population distribution does not matter. That is the power behind the Central Limit Theorem.

3.1 An Example:

As our first example, let's consider a population that consists of the numbers from 1 to 20. It follows that the population size, N, is 20, and the elements of the population are $N_1=1$, $N_2=2$, … $N_{20}=20$. This population has a mean and a standard deviation:

[Eq. 10]
$$\mu = \sum_{i=1}^{20} X_i / 20 = 10.5$$

[Eq. 11]
$$\sigma = \sqrt{\sum_{i=1}^{20} (x_i - 10.5)^2 / 20} = 5.766$$

Each element in the population has an equal probability of occurring, $1/N = .05$. So we can say the shape of the distribution is uniform, or rectangular (and decidedly not Normal.)

Let's see what happens when we construct sampling distributions of various sample sizes from this population. For a given sample size, n, the first interesting question is how many samples there are of size n we can take from the population. Before we can answer that we have to answer the question: are we sampling with or without replacement? For most practical sampling situations, we sample without replacement. But it is instructive to look at both cases.

3.1.1 With replacement: When we sample with replacement, we draw an element from the population, record its value, and then replace it. Therefore, the same element might be drawn into a sample more than once. A simple illustration of this is the throwing of dice. Assume we have a six-sided die (N=6). We toss it once, record its value (from 1 to 6), and then toss it again. Thus we could get two 6's, or maybe a 4 and a 3. This is the same situation as throwing two dice once; the possible outcomes are the same. But if we think of it as throwing one die twice, it is more intuitive that we are doing so with replacement.

There are six ways the first toss can come out. There are six ways the second toss can come out. So the total number of possible outcomes is 36 (6^2, or N^n). But this number means that the combination of 4,3 is *different* from the combination 3,4. It is the number of outcomes *with replacement with regard for order*. If we want to consider 4,3 and 3,4 to be the *same* outcome (*without regard for order*) the formula for the number of outcomes is more complex:

[Eq. 12]
$$outcomes = (N+n-1)!/(N-1)!(n!) = 21$$

3.1.2 Without replacement: In most practical sampling problems we sample without replacement. That is, we draw one element from the population, record it, then draw another. It is not possible for the same element to be drawn more than once.

There are N ways to draw the first element. There are N-1 elements remaining, so there are N-1 ways to draw the second element. So there are N(N-1) ways to draw the first two elements. Therefore there are N(N-1)(N-2)---(N-n+1) ways to draw the n elements. But this is **with regard for order**. That is drawing X_5 and X_7 …… is *different* from drawing X_7 and X_5 ….. in our sample. If we want to look at the number of combinations *without regard for order*, we need to remove the order from the n elements in the sample. We do that by recognizing there are n ways to order the first element of the sample, for each one of those there are n-1 ways to order the second element, etc. So we can calculate the number of ways to order n elements of the sample as n(n-1)(n-2)---(3)(2)(1). So the total number of possible samples is:

$$samples = \frac{N(N-1)(N-2)---(N-n+1)}{n(n-1)(n-2)---(3)(2)(1)}$$

[Eq. 13]

This is valid, but it can be simplified (sort of). Multiply both numerator and denominator by (N-n)(N-n-1)---3*2*1. This will result in the standard formula for combinations:

$$C(N,n) = \frac{N!}{n!(N-n)!}$$

[Eq. 14]

We can read this as saying the total number of samples (combinations) of size n we can draw from a population of size N (without regard for order) is C(N,n) or the number of combinations of N items taken n at a time.

UltraCAD has introduced a calculator that can do these types of calculations quite easily. It is illustrated in Figure 1 for the case of our population (N=20) and a sample size of n=3, showing that there are 1,140 individual samples of size 3 that can be drawn from a population of 20.

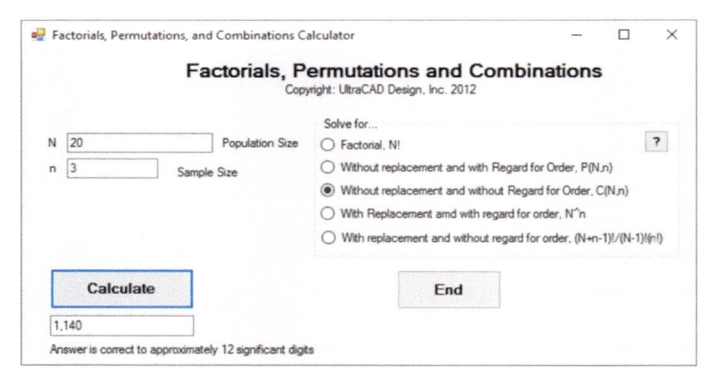

Figure 1
Calculator for permutations and combinations.
available at:
http://www.ultracad.com/calc.htm

3.2 Back to the Example.

Appendix 1 shows sampling distributions for all sample sizes from 1 to 20 for our population of 20 elements. There are 20 samples of size 1. There are 190 samples of size 2, as many as 1,140 samples of size 3, and so on up to 184,756 samples of size 10. A computer was used to determine how many sample means of each sample size fell into the categories in the left hand column. For example, the left column shows that of the 1,140 possible samples of size 3, four of them had means between 2.0 and 2.99. Another 114 of them had means between 8.0 and 8.99. And 180 of them had means between 10.0 and 11.0.

Technical note: It is desirable that the table be symmetrical around the population mean, 10.5. Therefore, the lower boundaries of the ranges below 10.5 are exact integers, while the upper boundaries of the ranges above 10.5 are exact integers. This is why, for n=1, there is a slight discontinuity exactly in the center.

There are some very informative conclusions that can be drawn from inspecting Appendix 1. First note that the mean of the worst possible sample that can be drawn at any sample size gets closer to the true population mean as the sample size increases. The worst sample mean from a sample of size 2 lies in the range 1.0 to 1.99 (or from 19.01 to 20). The worst sample mean from a sample of size 5 lies in the range 3.0 to 3.99. The worst sample mean from a sample of size 9 lies in the range 5.0 to 5.99. And the probability of selecting the worst possible sample goes down as sample size increases; from one in 190 for n=2, one in 15,504 for n=5, and one in 167,960 for n=9. It is very important to note that the *worst possible* sample mean moves closer to the true population mean as n increases, and the probability of selecting that worst possible sample mean drops dramatically.

Second, even though the sample means get closer to the true population mean as n increases, and therefore the sample mean becomes a more reliable estimate of the population mean, it does not mean that sample mean will actually equal the population mean. The second row at the bottom of Table 1 shows how many sample means actually equal the population mean for each sample size. Note, for example, that for n=13 all the 77,520 sample means are somewhat close to the population mean, but *none* of them actually equal the population mean.

Third, although we have not talked specifically about the Normal curve yet, simply looking at the sampling distribution for each sample size suggests by inspection that the sampling distribution becomes more and more "normal" as the sample size increases. Figure 2 illustrates this. *(Note: This is a normalized set of curves. That means each curve has been scaled such that the area under the curve = 1.0.)*

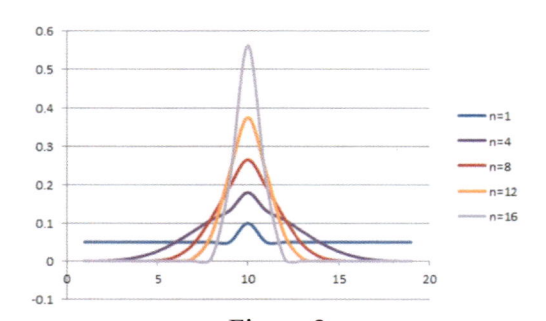

Figure 2
Note how the sampling distributions from Appendix 1 get closer to a normal curve as n increases.

3.3 The Normal Curve:

If we look at the sampling distribution relative frequency curve for sample size n=16 we can compare it to a standard Normal distribution with the same mean and standard deviation. This is done in Figure 3. Even though the sample size is only 16, and the population distribution is anything but a normal curve, nevertheless the approximation of the sampling distribution to a normal curve is pretty close. The Central Limit Theorem seems to be working!

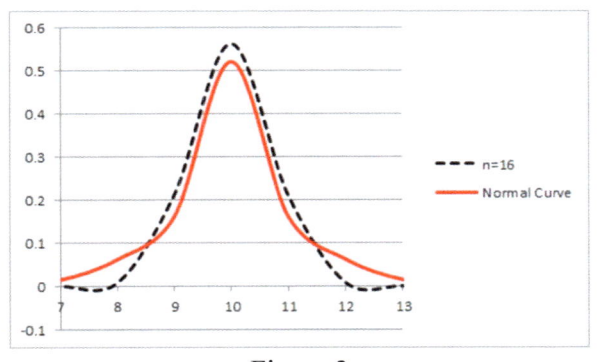

Figure 3
Comparing n=16 and a Normal curve.

Now here is why the fact that the sampling distribution approaches a normal curve is important. A Normal curve, with mean = 50 and standard deviation = 10, is shown in Figure 4. The vertical lines in the figure show the places that are +/- one and two standard deviations away from the mean. In a Normal curve, 68% of the elements of the population are within +/- one sigma (standard deviation) from the mean. 95% of the elements are within two sigma of the mean. As many as 99.7% of the observations are within +/- 3 sigma of the mean.

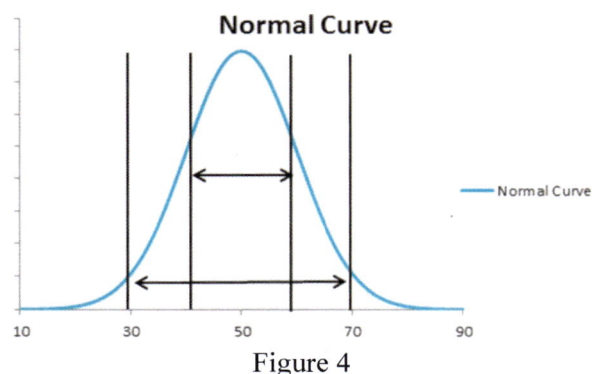

Figure 4
Normal curve with mean = 10 and sigma = 10.

If the sampling distribution (the distribution of the means of all the possible samples) is a Normal curve, I know that 95% of the time, the sample mean I have is within 2 standard deviations (two standard deviations of the sampling distribution, $\sigma_{\bar{x}}$) of the TRUE population mean I am trying to estimate.

So go back to my initial problem of estimating the average weight of the shipping containers passing through a terminal. Suppose I take a sample of 400 of the containers and find that the mean of the sample ($\bar{x}$) is 32,000 lbs. Suppose I calculate from the sample that the sample standard deviation is 6,000 lbs. This is an estimate of the population standard deviation, σ. If I divide that by the square root of the sample size, I get an estimate of the standard deviation of sampling distribution:

$$\sigma_{\bar{x}} = 6000 / \sqrt{400} = 300 \text{ lbs}$$

If the sampling distribution is a Normal curve with mean 32,000 lbs and a standard deviation of 300 lbs, then I know that the mean I selected from the sampling distribution was within +/- 600 lbs of the true population mean with a 95% confidence level. Or, expressed differently, I know that, with 95% confidence, the true population mean is within the range 32,000 +/- 600 lbs.

So I have now estimated the population mean (the mean weight of all the shipping containers), and I have a measure of confidence of how close my estimate is to the "truth," even though I started with no knowledge whatsoever of what the population parameters were, what the shape of it was, or even how many elements (N) were in it! Seems pretty powerful!

4. Sample Size:

Throughout this booklet we have used words like, "For sufficient sample size." So, specifically, what do we mean by that? How large a sample is "sufficient?"

4.1 For Normal Approximation:

If the population distribution is normally distributed, then the sampling distribution will be normally distributed for *any* sample size, including one. Any sample size will be "sufficient."

But if the population distribution is not normally distributed, then there is no particular rule about sample size. Except most authors and sources will say that a sample size of n=30 or n=40 is sufficient for the sampling distribution to be normally distributed regardless of the distribution of the population distribution. So in any situation where the population distribution is unknown, n=30 to n=40 is sufficient. (Personally, I tend to favor n=30.)

4.2 For Sufficient Precision:

The precision of the estimate (i.e. the value of sigma-x-bar), is the standard deviation of the population (sigma) divided by the square root of the sample size. But if we don't know anything about the population in the first place, how can we estimate the required sample size (for the required precision) without knowing sigma? There are several possible options available to us.

First, we may be able to estimate sigma based on a prior study. Second, an experienced statistician may be able to estimate it by experience, at least close enough to undertake the study. Third, we may do a pilot study with a smaller sample size specifically for the purpose of estimating sigma.

In any event, when we take the final sample, we calculate the standard deviation of the sample as an estimate of the population standard deviation. If our resulting sigma-x-bar is satisfactory, fine. If not, we continue sampling until a sufficiently large sample has been obtained.

5. Another Example:

Let's assume a population of the numbers from 00 to 99. So, $X_1=0, X_2=1, X_3=2,\ldots X_{99}=98, X_{100}=99$. Let each element of the population occur with equal probability, i.e. 1/100 or .01. The parameters of this population are (from Equations 1 and 2):

N=100

[Eq. 15]
$$\mu = \sum_{i=1}^{N} X_i / N = 49.5$$

[Eq. 16]
$$\sigma = \sqrt{\sum_{i=1}^{N} \left((X_i - \mu)^2 / N\right)} = 28.866$$

Assume we take 5,000 samples from this population and calculate the mean (x-bar) of each sample. These 5,000 sample x-bars approximate the sampling distribution. We will obviously do this experiment using a computer and a random number generator. And we will be sampling *with replacement,* because it is too hard to program the computer to run samples without replacement (at least for me!) We will group sample means within a range of one digit, i.e. between 0 to <1.0, 1.0 to <2.0. 2.0 to <3.0, etc.

Figure 5 (next page) shows the actual sample data for sample sizes along with a normal curve that fits the data:

n=1, (C(100,1) = 100 possible samples)
n=3, (C(100,3) = 161,700 possible samples)
n=10, (C(100,10) approximately = 1.73×10^{13} possible samples)
n=50, (C(100,50) approximately = 1.0089×10^{29} possible samples.)

The number of combinations for each sample size was calculated using the calculator shown in Figure 1.

6. Extension to Proportions:

Suppose we want to know what proportion of a population favors a particular candidate in a coming election. Here there are only two possible outcomes (favor or don't favor) and perhaps a few with "no opinion."

This type of population has the parameters:

Size = N
Proportion for = π
Proportion against = 1 - π
Variance = $\pi * (1 - \pi)$

Standard deviation = $\sqrt{\pi(1-\pi)}$

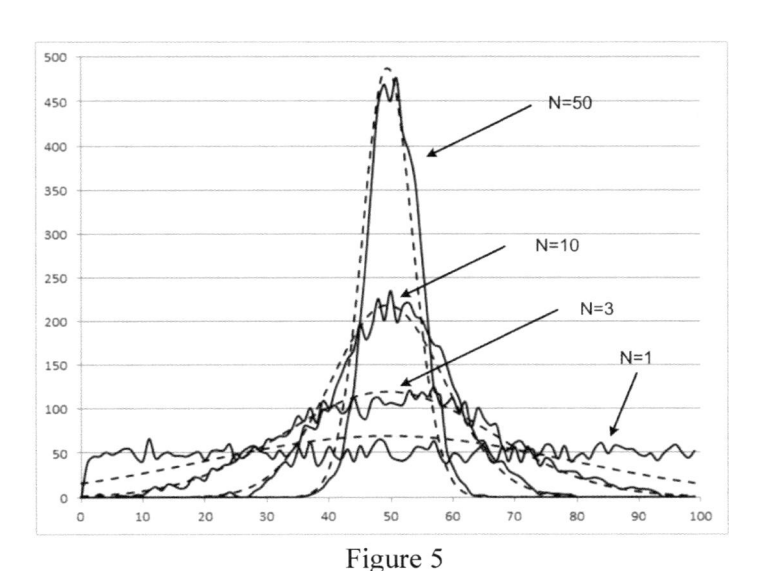

Figure 5
As sample size increases, the sampling distribution approaches a Normal curve more closely. (Solid line equals sample data, dotted line is Normal approximation for the same sample size.)

If we take a sample from this population, of size n, we can obtain an estimate of the population proportion, p, and a standard deviation of that estimate equal to:

[Eq. 17]
$$\sigma_p = \sqrt{(p(1-p))/(n-1)}$$

The estimate we obtain, p, is one element from the sampling distribution from this population of size n. The Central Limit Theorem applies here, too, so the sampling distribution is approximated with a Normal curve whose mean is π (the population proportion) and whose standard deviation is given by Equation 17.

So suppose I sample 3,000 people from a population and ask them their preference for a particular candidate. Suppose the sample proportion is p=.45 (45 percent in favor of this candidate.) What can I conclude from this sample?

If I have followed good sampling procedures, I can conclude that the true proportion of the population that supports this candidate is within +/- two standard deviations from the sample proportion, or

$$\pi = .45 \pm 2\sqrt{.45(.55)/3000} = .45 \pm .0180$$

That is, my sample estimate should be a little better than +/- 2%.

We can use a computer simulation similar to the one above to verify that the sampling distribution for proportions also looks like a Normal curve (for sufficiently large samples.) Suppose we take samples from a population where the population proportion is .45 for (.55 against) a particular candidate or proposition. Let's take samples (again with replacement, for simplicity) of size 100. Figure 6 plots the results of the sample, along with the normal curve approximating it.

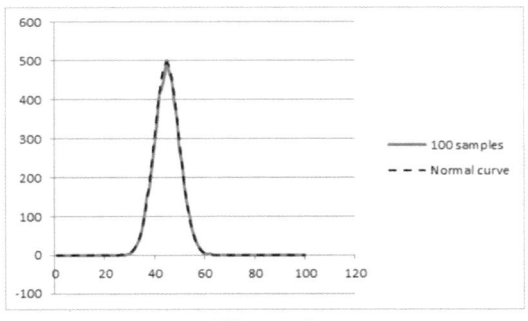

Figure 6
Sampling distribution for a proportion = .45 and n=100.

The fit to a normal curve is almost perfect!

But if we look at this size sample from another way, plotting the sampling distributions for both those for and against,

31

there is a significant overlap between the two curves, shown in Figure 7. That is, if we want to conclude whether this population approves or disapproves the proposition, a sample size of n=100 is somewhat likely to lead to an error!

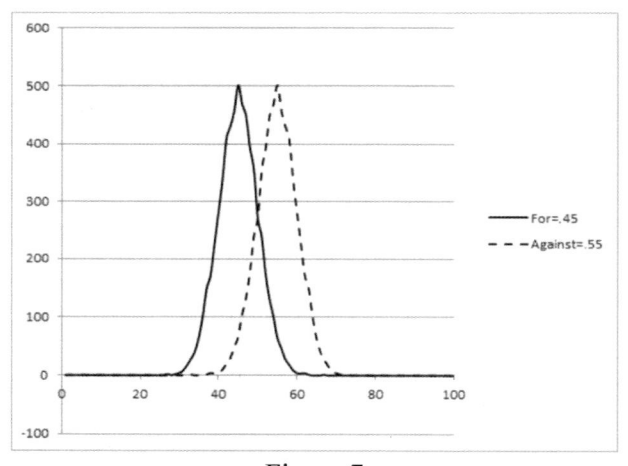

Figure 7
The sampling distributions for "approve" (.45) and "disapprove" (.55) have a significant overlap.

On the other hand, if we increase the sample size, the precision of the estimate gets much better. Figure 8 shows the results for a sample size of 3,000, which safely discriminates between the two positions in this population.

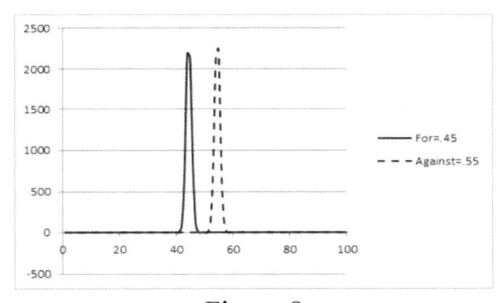

Figure 8
Same data as Figure 7 for n=3,000

Note that the variance for a proportion near 50% is much larger than that for a lower percentage. Simply note that .5*.5=.25 while .9*.1=.09. Thus, the sample size needed for a given precision is larger if the proportion is near 50% than it would be if the proportion were higher or lower. Nevertheless, an assumed variance of .25 is often chosen as a starting point in these types of sampling problems for conservatism.

6.1 Margin of Error:

We routinely hear news reports that provide a sample percentage in favor of some issue or candidate, with a note that "the margin of error equals ..." The term "margin of error" is one of the most misused and misunderstood terms used in journalism! Here is what it *should* mean:

The margin of error is one-half the confidence interval.

Two points are of interest:

First, the definition references a confidence interval. When was the last time you saw a level of confidence (68%, 90%, 99%, etc.) specified in the same sentence as the term "margin of error?" I don't think I ever have. Therefore, the term is somewhat undefined.

Second, (for 95% confidence) the confidence interval (for a normal distribution) is +/- two-sigma wide. So the margin of error is +/- two sigma, or simply two sigma. In the example above, my sample of size 3,000 found a population proportion of .45 with a sampling standard deviation of .009. The two-sigma confidence interval was +/- .018. So, at 95%, the margin of error would be 1.8% or +/- 1.8%.

So here is what we should be able to understand:

1. If the level of confidence is unstated, we should be able to assume a level of 95% confidence. (Do you trust that?)
2. The stated margin of error (assuming 95%) should be two times the standard deviation of the sampling distribution.
3. For the previous statements to be true, the sample taken should be a truly random, unbiased sample of the appro-

priate size taken from the specified target population. (Do you trust that?)

4. Care should have been taken in the sample design to avoid interjecting any other bias, such as bias in the wording of the questions. (Do you trust that?)

The reason that I interject the question of trust is that you almost never see reported (a) a specified level of confidence, (b) any type of reference as to *HOW* the sample was taken, or (c) the specific wording of the question being asked.

Simply look at the results of samples on a given topic provided by Republicans and by Democrats. Then decide if you can really trust any of them!

# Appendix 1
N=20
Mean = 10.5, Standard deviation = 5.766

These tables list the sampling distributions for a population of 20 (N=20) elements (1, 2, 3, ... 19, 20) each with an equal probability of occurring. Sampling distributions are shown, along with key statistics, for sample sizes (n) from 1 to 20.

You can download a larger image of Appendix 1 formatted for an 8.5x11 page in landscape mode from http://www.ultracad.com/combinations/appendix1.pdf .

Sigma-x-bar employs the finite population correction factor:

$$\sigma_{\bar{x}} = \left(\frac{\sigma_x}{\sqrt{n}}\right)\sqrt{\frac{N-n}{n-1}}$$

See the technical note in Section 2.2

Sample Size	n=1	n=2	n=3	n=4	n=5	n=6	n=7	n=8	n=9	n=10
Sample Mean Between	abs f (rel f)	abs f (rel f)	abs f (rel f)	abs f (rel f)	abs f (rel f)	abs f (rel f)	abs f (rel f)	abs f (rel f)	abs f (rel f)	abs f (rel f)
1.0-1.99	1 0.0500	1 0.0053								
2.0-2.99	1 0.0500	3 0.0158	4 0.0035	2 0.0004						
3.0-3.99	1 0.0500	5 .0.263	12 0.0105	16 0.0033	12 0.0008	4 0.0001				
4.0-4.99	1 0.0500	7 0.0368	25 0.0219	53 0.0109	71 0.0046	60 0.0015	30 0.0004	7 0.0001		
5.0-5.99	1 0.0500	9 0.0474	42 0.0368	123 0.0254	241 0.0155	324 0.0084	298 0.0038	181 0.0014	67 0.0004	12 0.0001
6.0-6.99	1 0.0500	11 0.0579	64 0.0561	236 0.0487	595 0.0384	1080 0.0279	1438 0.0186	1402 0.0111	980 0.0058	468 0.0025
7.0-7.99	1 0.0500	13 0.0684	90 0.0789	382 0.0788	1144 0.0738	2552 0.0658	4336 0.0559	5670 0.0450	5705 0.0340	4363 0.0236
8.0-8.99	1 0.0500	15 0.0789	114 0.1000	529 0.1092	1792 0.1156	4588 0.1184	9126 .01177	14353 0.1139	17999 0.1072	18016 0.0975
9.0-9.99	1 0.0500	17 0.0895	129 0.1132	645 0.1331	2347 0.1514	6490 0.1674	14125 0.1822	24649 0.1957	34900 0.2078	40347 0.2184
10.0-11.0	1 0.0500	28 0.1474	180 0.1579	873 0.1802	3100 0.1999	8564 0.2209	18814 0.2427	33446 0.2655	48658 0.2897	58344 0.3158
11.01-12.0	1 0.0500	17 0.0895	129 0.1132	645 0.1331	2347 0.1514	6490 0.1674	14125 0.1822	24649 0.1957	34900 0.2078	40347 0.2184
12.01-13.0	1 0.0500	15 0.0789	114 0.1000	529 0.1092	1792 0.1156	4588 0.1184	9126 .01177	14353 0.1139	17999 0.1072	18016 0.0975
13.01-14.0	1 0.0500	13 0.0684	90 0.0789	382 0.0788	1144 0.0738	2552 0.0658	4336 0.0559	5670 0.0450	5705 0.0340	4363 0.0236
14.01-15.0	1 0.0500	11 0.0579	64 0.0561	236 0.0487	595 0.0384	1080 0.0279	1438 0.0186	1402 0.0111	980 0.0058	468 0.0025
15.01-16.0	1 0.0500	9 0.0474	42 0.0368	123 0.0254	241 0.0155	324 0.0084	298 0.0038	181 0.0014	67 0.0004	12 0.0001
16.01-17.0	1 0.0500	7 0.0368	25 0.0219	53 0.0109	71 0.0046	60 0.0015	30 0.0004	7 0.0001		
17.01-18.0	1 0.0500	5 .0.263	12 0.0105	16 0.0033	12 0.0008	4 0.0001				
18.01-19.0	1 0.0500	3 0.0158	4 0.0035	2 0.0004						
19.01-20.0	1 0.0500	1 0.0053								
Total # means	20	190	1,140	4,845	15,504	38,760	77,520	125,970	167,960	184,756
Means exactly 10.5	0	10	0	177	0	1,242	0	3,788	0	5,448
% exactly 10.5	0.00	5.26	0.00	3.65	0.00	3.20	0.00	3.01	0.00	2.95
sigma x-bar	5.766	3.969	3.149	2.646	2.291	2.021	1.803	1.620	1.462	1.323

Sample Size	n=11	n=12	n=13	n=14	n=15	n=16	n=17	n=18	n=19	n=20
Sample Mean Between	abs f (rel f)	abs f (rel f)	abs f (rel f)	abs f (rel f)	abs f (rel f)	abs f (rel f)	abs f (rel f)	abs f (rel f)	abs f (rel f)	abs f (rel f)
1.0-1.99										
2.0-2.99										
3.0-3.99										
4.0-4.99										
5.0-5.99										
6.0-6.99	138 0.0008	19 0.0002								
7.0-7.99	2468 0.0147	980 0.0078	246 0.0032	30 0.0008						
8.0-8.99	14305 0.0852	8881 0.0705	4197 0.0541	1438 0.0371	324 0.0209	38 0.0078				
9.0-9.99	38149 0.2271	29415 0.2335	18349 0.2367	9126 0.2354	3531 0.2277	1021 0.2107	204 0.1789	25 0.1316		
10.0-11.0	57840 0.3444	47380 0.3761	31936 0.4120	17572 0.4534	7794 0.5027	2727 0.5628	732 0.6421	140 0.7368	20 1.0000	1 1.0000
11.01-12.0	38149 0.2271	29415 0.2335	18349 0.2367	9126 0.2354	3531 0.2277	1021 0.2107	204 0.1789	25 0.1316		
12.01-13.0	14305 0.0852	8881 0.0705	4197 0.0541	1438 0.0371	324 0.0209	38 0.0078				
13.01-14.0	2468 0.0147	980 0.0078	246 0.0032	30 0.0008						
14.01-15.0	138 0.0008	19 0.0002								
15.01-16.0										
16.01-17.0										
17.01-18.0										
18.01-19.0										
19.01-20.0										
Total # means	167,960	125,970	77,520	38,760	15,504	4,845	1,140	190	20	1
Means exactly 10.5	0	3,788	0	1,242	0	177	0	10	0	1
% exactly 10.5	0	3.01	0.00	3.20	0.00	3.65	0.00	5.26	0.00	100.00
sigma x-bar	1.197	1.080	0.971	0.866	0.764	0.661	0.556	0.441	0.303	0

ABOUT THE AUTHOR:

Douglas Brooks has a BS/EE and an MS/EE from Stanford and a PhD from the University of Washington. He has held positions on two faculties, teaching (among other things) Statistics and Quantitative Methods. In the business world he has held positions in engineering and marketing management, general management, and as an owner of three corporations.

For the last 20 years he has owned a small engineering service firm and written numerous technical articles on Printed Circuit Board Design and Signal Integrity issues, and has published one book. He has given seminars several times a year all over the US, as well as Moscow, China, Taiwan, Japan, and Canada. His primary focus is on making complex technical issues easily understood by those without advanced degrees.

Brooks' corporate web pages are at:
http://www.ultracad.com

Printed in Great Britain
by Amazon